P(

The Inclusive Church Resource

DARTON · LONGMAN + TODD

First published in Great Britain in 2014 by
Darton, Longman and Todd Ltd
1 Spencer Court
140 – 142 Wandsworth High Street
London SW18 4JJ

ISBN 978-0-232-53068-1

A catalogue record for this book is available from the
British Library

Phototypeset by Judy Linard
Printed and bound in Great Britain by
Page Bros, Norwich, Norfolk

Contents

Acknowledgements

Inclusive Church is grateful to all who have made this book possible.

In particular we would like to acknowledge the enthusiasm and support for this book from David Moloney at Darton, Longman and Todd.

We are grateful to the Churches Equality Practitioner Group for ideas and suggestions for this book series

We would especially like to thank those who have generously given of their time and contributed stories, reflections and resources for this book.

We are grateful to St Bride's Liverpool, Church Action on Poverty and the Student Christian Movement for their assistance in this book.

It is our hope that all that is shared here will encourage others to go further in the work of creating a more inclusive and welcoming church.

About Inclusive Church

Inclusive Church was formed in 2003. From the start, churches and individuals have signed up to the statement of belief as a way of indicating their desire to see a more accepting and open church.

The Inclusive Church 'Statement of Belief'

We believe in inclusive church – church which does not discriminate, on any level, on grounds of economic power, gender, mental health, physical ability, race or sexuality. We believe in church which welcomes and serves all people in the name of Jesus Christ; which is scripturally faithful; which seeks to proclaim the Gospel afresh for each generation; and which, in the power of the Holy Spirit, allows all people to grasp how wide and long and high and deep is the love of Jesus Christ.

www.inclusive-church.org

Introduction
SAVITRI HENSMAN

*Savitri Hensman, an Inclusive Church trustee
with lead responsibility on economic exclusion,
was born in Sri Lanka and lives in London.
She is a writer, activist, Ekklesia associate
and works in the voluntary sector.*

Many communities are now a patchwork of pawnbrokers and chic boutiques, high-priced properties and social housing (like the estate where I live). Even in mainly prosperous areas, there are often pockets of poverty. Economic exclusion is an issue which confronts Christians in the UK and beyond.

Growing economic inequality within and among neighbourhoods has meant that sizeable numbers of people are excluded from full participation. At the most basic level, a newborn boy in East Dorset can expect to live seven years longer than one in Blaenau Gwent,[1]

---

[1] *Life expectancy at birth and at age 65 by local areas in England and Wales, 2010– 12*, Office for National Statistics, 24 October 2013, http://www.ons.gov.uk/ons/publications/re-reference-tables.html?edition=tcm%3A77-326676.

while newborn girls in the most advantaged areas in England are likely to spend twenty more years of their lives in good health than those in the most deprived areas.[2]

Concern about poor people being marginalised in church and society is not new. Almost two thousand years ago, the Epistle of James warned against snobbery towards worse-off churchgoers and pointed out the injustices of the rich. Other early Christian leaders too were strongly critical of class hierarchy and mistreatment of the poor. However (with some exceptions), church leaders later came to accept deep economic and social divisions, while encouraging charitable giving. In recent centuries however, many Christians worldwide have become involved in trying to understand and tackle the causes of poverty.

In modern Europe, poverty has sometimes been treated as a problem which only affects far-off countries and a handful of unfortunate or idle people closer to home. This was never true and, in recent years, it has become

[2] *Inequality in Healthy Life Expectancy at Birth by National Deciles of Area Deprivation: England, 2009–11*, Office for National Statistics, 14 March 2014, http://www.ons.gov. uk/ons/rel/disability-and-health-measurement/inequality-in-healthy-life-expectancy-at-birth-by-national-deciles-of-area-deprivation--england/2009-11/stb---inequality-in-hle. html#tab-Key-Findings.

increasingly apparent. Numerous households have been plunged into stark poverty. Even people in paid work often struggle to pay for basics; indeed more than half of the 13 million people living in poverty in the UK in 2011/12 were in a working family.[3] Debt, cold, homelessness and hunger are taking a heavy toll and 900,000 people received help from food banks in 2013/14.[4] The impact is often made worse by stigma, especially against people in need of social security. Many in local churches, their families or neighbours live precariously, so that an unexpected bill or slight drop in pay can plunge them into crisis – though sometimes, out of fear or shame, they will hide their plight from all but a handful of people.

Economic hardship is often combined with other forms of disadvantage. For instance, many women, disabled people, members of certain ethnic minority communities and lesbian, gay, bisexual, transgender and intersex people who have been displaced from their homes are on low incomes. How Christians (whether

---

[3] *Monitoring poverty and social exclusion 2013*, Joseph Rowntree Foundation, 8 December 2013, http://www.jrf.org.uk/publications/monitoring-poverty-and-social-exclusion-2013.

[4] Trussell Trust statistics, http://www.trusselltrust.org/stats.

poor, rich or in between) respond to economic exclusion also ties in with broader questions of what love and justice mean in a world of inequality and of our vision of the church.

Gradually Inclusive Church, while continuing to tackle the obvious ways in which certain groups have been excluded from types of ministry and celebration of loving relationships, has also begun to address other issues, including poverty. This has included information-sharing and signposting to projects and initiatives focusing on economic exclusion.

A survey of member churches in 2013 found that most believed that poverty was on the rise in their neighbourhoods, though sometimes this went with social polarisation: 'In some parts of the community [poverty is] increasing, in other parts people are getting wealthier.'

There were varying views among Inclusive Church contact persons on how high a priority economic exclusion was for their congregations, and also on whether these congregations fully accept people facing economic exclusion, including in leadership positions. Most of those who responded believed that poverty should be a high priority for Inclusive Church as a whole, though some recognised that resources might limit what could be done.

It was pointed out that class differences

meant that worshippers in areas with high levels of deprivation were not always aware of their neighbours' needs. At the same time, being in a church community, many of whose members were educationally disadvantaged, refugees or struggling just to get by, brought its own challenges.

In response to the survey, Inclusive Church produced various online resources, including facts and figures on poverty in the UK, prayer and worship materials and sources of further information.[5] This book will also become a valuable resource for churches as they seek to be better informed about issues related to poverty.

Meanwhile at national level, several churches continued to highlight issues of poverty, including exposing harmful myths spread by politicians and the media about the poor,[6] while senior clergy, like the Archbishop of Canterbury, highlighted problems such as high-interest lending and food poverty, encouraging policy changes as well as practical action.

Churches have not always been good at listening to the voices of poor people themselves

5   Poverty: Inclusive Church website, http://www.inclusive-church.org/node/569.

6   *Truth and lies about poverty*, Baptist Union of Great Britain, Methodist Church, Church of Scotland and United Reformed Church, 2013, http://www.jointpublicissues.org.uk/truthandliesaboutpoverty/

and making sure that these are heard, backing struggles led by those most affected by economic exclusion and asking tough questions about the workings of a society which result in stark differences of wealth, prestige and power.

The problem of poverty in the UK continues to grow, with reports of increasing numbers of desperate people turning to food banks and tragedies as some people whose benefits have been cut die not long afterwards. Often people who are vulnerable because of sickness, bereavement or other forms of loss find their suffering worsened because of material hardship and prejudice.

This book contains personal stories – a reminder that, behind statistics and analyses, important as these are, there are human beings and networks of connection – and looks at key theological issues.

It is easy even for Christians seeking to be compassionate and inclusive to think in terms of 'them' and 'us': either that 'we', the not-so-poor, must rescue the needy or that 'we', the poor, must rely on others who are seen by the world as more worthy and influential. However, a different way of thinking and acting can lead to the breaking down of barriers and radical transformation of church and society, bringing, in James's phrase, a harvest of righteousness.

PART 1

Experience

Stories from lived experience are central to this book. It would be easy to skip this section and read the theological reflection or look at the resources. The stories here are real and speak of what it is like to live with poverty in different forms. These are stories of how individuals, churches and communities, at home and in other parts of the world, respond to the reality of poverty.

We are grateful to these storytellers for their honesty. Our theological reflection and practical outworking should follow from these accounts of lived experience, so please take time to read these stories carefully.

Cate's story

Cate Jacobs has been attending St Bride's Liverpool for about 3 years. She is 51, mother of 3, grandmother of 4 and a poet. She has been living with HIV for 19 years and previously wrote a column for Positively Women *magazine and* Positive Nation. *Her book* Climbing Mountains in the Dark *is due to be republished as an e-book later this year.*

My initial reaction when I was asked to write this piece was 'but I'm not poor!', although in reality I fit the poverty profile.

I have been in receipt of Employment and Support Allowance since I was made redundant and became homeless in 2008. My mental health went into a tailspin, along with a decline in my physical health, as I struggled through nine months of homelessness. I was house-sitting for friends and sofa surfing where I could, to keep myself out of hostels and off the streets. In February 2009 I was finally offered appropriate housing and I moved into an empty flat, with few possessions to furnish it with and no grants available to help me. For months I slept on the floor because I had no bed; rebuilding and decorating my home was a long, slow process.

During that time I found it very hard to reach out to others or even admit the level of poverty I lived with. It crushes my dignity every time I have to acknowledge it and over the years I have become a dab hand at disguising it from others; I've had plenty of practice. I've existed on a low income all of my adult life as a result of a divorce and single-parenting three children, while living with a long-term chronic condition that affects my ability to work, but not sufficiently for me to qualify for Disability Living Allowance.

Winter is always hard – there is never enough money on the meter to stay warm, and often I will make a hot-water bottle and go back to bed rather than be up and have the heating on. Last winter I ended up with flu and the year before I had pneumonia! In between I fell foul of the bedroom tax and had to move.

I am great at the 'shabby chic' look, and am a whizz at creating a feast out of the next-to-nothing ingredients in my cupboards. I was lucky. When I was young I learnt from my mother how to make tasty, nutritious and filling meals and it saved my children from going hungry, although that wasn't always true for me. Soup was a daily part of our diet and a way of ensuring nothing went to waste. I had a big 100-year-old pot that bubbled away on my stove throughout the year. This may sound comforting and homely, but let me tell you I'd never choose 'soup of the day' from a menu. Soup was every day and poor food to me. So please don't give me soup!

My reality is that every choice I make is a compromise to another aspect of my budget – a tin of paint for the walls means less food in the fridge. I can only have a new pair of shoes or a haircut if I miss a utility payment. Birthdays and Christmas are an expense I dread. I am an expert at 'robbing Peter to pay Paul', but I'm often only three loaves of bread away from needing to go to the food bank. I've never used it because it is run from our church and the indignity of walking through the door would crucify me.

Because of the side-effects of the medication I take, I recently had to come to accept that I may never be capable of working again. My health is too erratic. I have no pension plan or any savings. All this is beginning to sound like a very bleak story and indeed it feels bleak if I focus on it for any length of time.

There is a gentle awareness among my

friends at church of my financial position and there is a subtle kindness that is extended to me in a variety of ways. I was given a bursary to enable me to go on a pilgrimage with our church community; people have been kind enough to gift me places on courses, taken me out for a meal as their guest, and I was given a crisis payment one winter. It is wonderful and I am truly grateful for these things, but the underlying issue of my financial poverty is as chronic as the illness I live with – it never goes away.

Poverty is embarrassing for the rich and the poor alike. I often experience people justifying what they have when they're around me, as if they are apologising for having more than me. I am happy that you're warm, can afford to go on holiday, buy a new car or whatever. I wouldn't want you to be without, any more than I want to be without myself. I guess what it highlights are the inequalities in which wealth is distributed in our world and how we value and measure people's contributions to society in general and therefore how we reward them.

It is a relief to me that the collection plate isn't passed among us on a Sunday morning, but left on the coffee bar. I don't have spare change to give to the church. What I have to offer is my time, my commitment, my energy, my creativity, my love and the warmest hug you're likely to get – which also happen to be the most precious resources I have to give. It has taken me a long time to see these as being as valuable to the life of the church as financial giving, and to leave my purse at home on Sundays.

Poverty is a global issue. It's an issue of the distribution of resources; wealth, food, water, medicine and land. It's going to take a fundamental shift in consciousness to eliminate poverty; and I pray for that. Somewhere in the Gospels Jesus said that the poor would be with us always – well, I think it would be an amazing legacy to prove him wrong! But will we?

I am poor because you are rich. For you and I to reach a place of equality and fairness, where both of us can afford our lives without struggle, it might require you to be willing to level down; which is radical and scary for those with more to lose financially. Individually we can only do what we can do – but I would suggest that includes looking carefully at the policies of the political parties we vote for and being aware of the implications our votes have on others, not just ourselves. Do we as church proactively support motions to eliminate third world debt? Poverty is political. Successive governments target the poorest in our society and we are scapegoated as scroungers and wastrels. Reality TV programmes are made that back up this prejudice.

Like many, I am just trying to get by day to day. Being long-term on benefits and poor was never my dream. It is wearing year in, year out to be juggling hot pennies. It erodes me. And yet if you asked me if I was poor, I'd say 'No!' Not only because in comparison to so many in our world or in our country, I am far from poor. I have a home, a bed to sleep in and food in my fridge. But I am rich in friends, family, love and spirit. It is the richness of my spiritual life that lifts me out of the poverty trap. For poverty only traps us when we see ourselves as being defined by our material wealth – it traps rich and poor alike, for different reasons. The glass half-full or half-empty is merely a matter of perspective, but I have to confess that a cup that runneth over would be nice from time to time – especially when the gas bill needs paying!

I'd like to live in a world where I wasn't reliant on handouts. I'd like to be part of a church where we not only preach a radical gospel but live it meaningfully in our everyday lives.

Victoria's story

Victoria Mason was born in England and grew up in Northern Ireland before studying history at Cambridge. Afterwards, she spent a year in Spain as an English Language Assistant and then returned to the UK to work as a Faith in Action intern for the Student Christian Movement. Victoria now works as Projects Coordinator for the Archbishop of Canterbury's Reconciliation Ministry, based in Coventry Cathedral.

One summer's day in 2012, I thought I was stepping outside for a general chat with a colleague. It turned out there was a hidden agenda: toilets. She was working, and I was volunteering, for the international development charity Concern Universal; and toilets were something about which she had plenty to say. The particular cause of her excitement was her recent discovery of the arborloo. This is what might be termed a moveable ecological toilet. It costs less than £3 to construct and consists primarily of a shallow pit, a concrete slab and a simple privacy structure. It serves as a private toilet for a year, after which it is moved to another location and the fertile soil left behind is used to grow abundant fruit trees. A brilliant idea.

But the main reason the conversation has stayed with me is because of what my colleague said next: the arborloo is not just creative, it is necessary. The earth cannot support the universal use of the flushable toilet which we use unthinkingly every day in the UK. It simply is not possible for everyone to do what I do and flush away 6–13 litres of fresh, clean water every time they go to the loo. But something needs to be done because one-third of human beings (2.5 billion people) do not even have access to a toilet that is clean or private, let alone one powered by gallons of drinkable water.

This is just one of the many faces of poverty in our world. Over the past year, I have had the opportunity to explore that thorny, controversial, vital issue of global poverty, working for the Student Christian Movement as a Faith in Action intern. The premise of the position is to work in a secular organisation, looking at – and reflecting theologically on – an issue of 'peace or justice' (global poverty in my case). For my placement, I returned to Concern Universal, this time as their Advocacy and Campaigns intern. It has been an opportunity for many new and exciting experiences. But, above all, it has been an opportunity to learn – about poverty on a global scale, about the role for the church in addressing it, and about the very question of who God is.

One of the primary lessons for me has been the realisation that there is, in fact, no such thing as 'global poverty'. Or, rather, there is no global experience of poverty. Poverty, wherever it occurs, is multifaceted, and it takes myriad different forms. It cannot be captured fully in the harrowing images of starving children with which we are all too familiar. Concern Universal works in nine countries across Africa, Asia and Latin America, but the meaning and the origins of poverty in each community are distinct. Their work in Brazil is concentrated in communities where poverty manifests itself in people's inability to be part of the decision-making that affects their lives (something fundamental to alleviating most types of poverty in most places). For Rashida, a schoolgirl in Bangladesh, poverty meant not being able to go to school because the school had no toilet or drinking-water facilities. Poverty for some girls and women in Malawi means spending hours each week walking in search of the firewood which allows them to cook, and thus neglecting education or paid work.

For many people, global poverty is synonymous with 'poor countries'. Another revelation for me this year has been the inadequacy of this idea. For one thing, in many places, pockets of extreme poverty rub shoulders with areas of great prosperity – the country is not uniformly rich or poor. This is the case in India, Brazil, China – and sometimes in the UK too. Nor are countries with very limited national wealth defined by their poverty. I have seen so often how varied and culturally rich 'poor countries' are. The sporting prowess of Brazil is an obvious example. Perhaps less obvious are the diverse musical traditions of Bangladesh or the fact that Rwanda has the largest number of women in parliament in the world. Many find it astounding to learn that Nigeria's 'Nollywood' produces more films each year than Hollywood, USA. Recognising the many dimensions of all countries not only gave me a more accurate vision of reality, but restored dignity and humanity to people so often lumped together as 'the world's poor'.

Starting my placement, I was well aware that global poverty was a highly contested issue. Doubts about the efficacy of providing aid to other countries, worries about corruption, the belief that 'charity begins at home' – all have been circulating for a long time. But, as the year went on, global poverty became an even hotter political potato. As January 2014 brought some of the wettest weather ever recorded and floods engulfed vast swathes of the UK, international aid came into the limelight once again. One newspaper launched a petition to demand that the UK aid budget be diverted to help those affected by flooding, echoing the calls of a prominent politician. It was this fervent debate, more than any other, with which I was continually grappling in all of my experiences and reflections. The more I wrestled with this, however, the more convinced I became of the human, political and theological imperative of tackling poverty on a global scale.

In seeking a scriptural perspective on the issue, I was repeatedly confronted with verses which framed poverty in the unexpected terms of justice and injustice. While generosity and charity certainly make their appearance in the Bible, at least as frequent are inducements to seek justice for the poor. Rather than encountering a God asking me to 'take pity', I found myself called to 'defend', 'uphold' and 'speak up'. '"He defended the cause of the poor and needy, and so all went well. Is that not what it means to know me?" declares the LORD' (Jeremiah 22:16, NIV). 'Learn to do right; seek justice. Defend the oppressed. Take up the cause

of the fatherless; plead the case of the widow'
(Isaiah 1:17, NIV). This affirms something that
I found to be true again and again: when we
look more deeply and critically at the reality of
poverty, we move from taking the stance that
'it is kind to help' to seeing that action is the
only moral option available to us. In short, we
go from viewing global poverty as a question of
charity to recognising it as one of justice.

For one thing, people across the world are
more interconnected than ever before. We
see it every day in the diversity of food in our
supermarkets, in the ease of communication
between countries thousands of miles apart, in
the international ubiquity of designer labels.
In milliseconds, we can access news stories
from almost any country. It is curious how
many people are willing to transgress every
geographical border to participate in this
global marketplace but then resolutely claim
the sacrosanctity of these same borders when
it comes to helping rather than buying. With
millions of lives touching each other every
minute, the distinctions between 'us' and 'them'
– which sustain an approach of charity without
solidarity – are increasingly untenable.

In this respect, current society is, or should
be, just catching up with the church, which has
had a globalised view of humanity from the

very beginning. Nowhere is this clearer than in the familiar image of the church as a body. Logically, when one part of that body is in pain, the only possible response of the other parts is not a sympathetic 'poor you', but rather a yelp of agony because the pain of one part and the pain of the body as a whole are inseparable. Surely a crucial role of the church in countering global poverty is simply to provide authentic witness to the common humanity shared by all.

Moreover, while some places are of course hotter or more ecologically volatile than others, I have seen that there is no inevitability about hunger, disease or disaster. It became increasingly apparent to me that global poverty was not merely the result of bad luck, but rather of human structures in which we all have a part to play.

While people are rightly scandalised by the existence of poverty in the United Kingdom, there can often be an unspoken assumption that hunger, disaster and disease in 'developing countries' are somehow inevitable. That it is because the climate of developing countries is intemperate. Or because developing countries are riddled with fault lines where earthquakes and tsunamis occur. Or because there just is less food and water there and there is nothing we can do about it. And the corollary of this perception is that any action we take is simply an act of generosity to people less fortunate than ourselves. I know that, without ever having been taught them explicitly, these were the ideas which underpinned my way of looking at poverty overseas.

The truth is, however, that there really is enough food to feed the world's population. Some African countries which suffer from severe malnutrition are also among the most fertile. Nor can we blame poverty on geography. Drought and desertification occur in Botswana and Niger alike; but Botswana has the eighth best ranking of any African country in the Human Development Index, at number 119, while Niger has the world's worst ranking at number 187. The World Bank offers the rather staggering statistic that low-income countries account for only 9 per cent of the world's disasters, but 48 per cent of the fatalities. Perhaps take a second to read that statistic again. It tells us that something more than nature is at play; and it tells us that poverty is an injustice rather than 'a pity'.

Of course, this injustice stems from many and varied sources. Knowledge of the crippling power of corrupt governments is one of the things which puts people off the idea of international aid in the first place. But it is not enough to blame foreign governments and leave it at that. Our own government – those who act by our vote and in our place – has a critical role in providing political and economic support to other governments internationally. Asking our governments to consider the human impact of their international deals and demanding that they be accountable is not a side project divorced from confronting the need 'on our doorstep'. It is part of the same vital process of ensuring that our politicians and authorities use their power fairly, transparently and with integrity, without which both our society and those around the world will be much poorer.

Poverty, moreover, is not just the product of governments. It is the result of multinational corporations who buy up swathes of land in that country and export everything they produce on it, draining money from the local economy. It is the result of the double standard which proclaims the right of UK workers to minimum standards of welfare, while embracing the cut-price, disposable consumer industry which allows workers in other countries to be exploited. It is the result of heavily industrialised nations contributing to 70 per cent of climate change, while poorer ones shoulder the burden. The gospel message which places the intrinsic value of people over the fleeting, and potentially corrupting, power of money has never been needed more.

Yet, in all of this, there is hope. Precisely because poverty is not inevitable, it can be conquered and injustice can be redressed. The arborloo is but one example of the many innovative, transformational, sustainable solutions being found. Organisations like Concern Universal are not providing temporary stopgaps but enabling people to find ways out of poverty that last. Women and men are starting businesses marketing shea butter, building fuel-efficient 'flower pot' stoves or selling vegetables. Communities are learning how to educate one another on sanitation and hygiene or on how to respond to floods. The interconnectedness of our world is making it easier for us all to be informed, to speak out, to hold those in power to account. 'Let justice roll on like a river, righteousness like a never-failing stream!' (Amos 5:24, NIV).

Ali's story

Ali Dorey works for the Diocese of Sheffield as Mission Development Coordinator for the North Sheffield Estates. She lives in a community house with two other single Christian women in Pitsmoor, a multicultural inner-urban area of Sheffield. 'There are no great acts, only small acts done with great love' (Mother Teresa) describes Ali's conviction about the mission of God.

Although I am writing my story in a book all about poverty, I am definitely not poor, at least not in the financial sense of the word. I was brought up in a leafy suburb of Bournemouth on the south coast of England, by parents who had bought their own property. Going back a generation, my dad's dad was a plumber, his mum was a housewife and they lived on a council estate in a slightly less leafy part of Bournemouth. My grandma on my dad's side was the only child of a miner from South Shields (in the North East) who had been crippled in a mining accident. Her mother worked in a local greengrocer's, and as soon as possible grandma left school and began work there too. Grandma and grandad met working in a factory that made radar equipment during the war.

My mum's dad served in the First World War, and always 'suffered with his nerves' afterwards, but worked as a company secretary for most of his life. Mum's mum had various office jobs and was a local councillor for a number of years. They owned their own home, and mum had a good education and trained to be a primary school teacher, which she did until she had children. She then gave up work to be a full-time mum, and through her considerable bargain-hunting skills, and a strong ethos of making do and mending, we had a good quality of life with just one breadwinner in the household.

I had an excellent education and no excuse not to thrive through my childhood. My brother and I both went on to university after completing our A levels. When my brother left university, before long he was earning the same wage my dad finished on after a lifetime working for the same company. Since I finished my first degree, I have only had short bouts of unemployment, in between which I've done some proofreading, community regeneration work, teaching and, more recently, become an ordained priest in the Church of England.

I first came to Sheffield as a student. Interestingly enough, it was my journey of faith that took me to a poorer part of the city initially. I quickly realised that the Christian Union at university and the big 'student churches' were full of gifted people. I felt instinctively that it was wrong for so much gifting to be located in one place, so I looked around for a small local church where I could be more 'useful'. I visited St John's Park, on the Wybourn estate to the south of the city, as some fellow students had run a holiday club there, and all the estate kids who'd come were involved in the Sunday service. In the service, the students led the kids doing the 'funky chicken' dance and various other crazy things. Then the vicar invited anyone from the small congregation who felt like they wanted to say something in response to come to the front. A man with tumours all over his face and one remaining arm ambled painfully to the front of church with the aid of a stick. Once he'd caught his breath he simply said, 'Well, I think it's brilliant what they've done, and it's great to see these kids here.' I was overwhelmed by the sight of someone in so much pain demonstrating so much grace and joy at what God was doing. When I went for coffee after the service, I was passing the hatch when someone threw a cloth at me and said, 'Give that a wipe will you, love?' And I knew I was home.

I stayed worshipping at St John's Park for about nine years, and in that time learnt more about who God is than I think I'd ever learnt before. It was a place of formation; I went there thinking I had something to give, but soon realised the boot was on the other foot. It was a place where my poverty began to be highlighted to me – my lack of community, specifically. I began to admire the local people at St John's for the sense of community that came naturally to them, and they became my surrogate family, in a way. I got a job working in the local community, and it became obvious to me that most people there had not had the privileged upbringing that I had. It was a whole world that I'd been largely ignorant of. And maybe because I was so close to my dad's mum, the miner's daughter, I began to really cherish local people, and the homespun wisdom I found in working-class cultures in Sheffield.

Fast-forwarding through a number of years (including a curacy in Askern, an ex-mining village in Doncaster) to 2011, I was licensed as a mission priest to work on a large group of estates in North Sheffield made up of predominantly social housing. About a year after I had started in this role, there were various discussions about the potential for a piece of work looking at the impact of the Government's welfare reform programme. A gifted social researcher who was a church member not far from my area had developed a tried-and-tested methodology for holding structured conversations that would enable us to gather useful information about the impact of welfare reform on people's lives in the more deprived parts of the city. The methodology was an empowering one (using Asset-Based Community Development), enabling interviewees to also be interviewers, and it built on the natural propensity of many local Sheffielders to tell their story.

We decided to pilot this project, which we named 'Listen Up', in a couple of estates in Sheffield, and then to roll it out to other areas in the diocese. I was involved in the pilot phase, with St Leonard's church on the Longley estate in North Sheffield, and then in the later phase on Southey estate, in partnership with Parson Cross Initiative (a local organisation set up by the Methodist Church to develop mission and community in some estates in North Sheffield).

In the pilot phase of Listen Up, a few volunteers from St Leonard's Longley congregation, one from the local tenants' association, a Methodist lay community development worker and I were trained up to participate. During the training, we had to practise holding the structured conversations with one another. I was one of the practice 'interviewees' at one point. I was already very aware of the wealth and poverty gap between me and potential other participants in Listen Up, but I realised that it was important for me to talk about my finances in the same way we would invite others to talk about theirs, to at least partly redress any power imbalance from the start.

When we came to doing the structured conversations, we found incredible openness in the people we listened to. It was quite hard to find people who weren't suspicious that we were from the Department of Work and Pensions, checking up on them, but the church connection by and large helped people to be less suspicious. Once people had agreed to engage with Listen Up, they were very open about their livelihoods and shared with us a lot of their strategies for survival. We also quickly realised how far they were from the stereotypical 'scrounger' that people on benefits were being portrayed as by some of the national press.

Listening to people's stories was frightening because, for most of them, things had happened that could easily happen to anyone, especially given the current economic climate. In most cases, major life events that were totally out of people's control had conspired to mean that they had ended up on benefits. Most of them also struggled with long-term health problems themselves or within their close family unit, which seriously affected their ability to earn enough money to survive.

I mainly paired up with the volunteer from the local tenants' association to do the structured conversations. During one conversation, the woman we were listening to, who had gone from being a professional, single woman to being a married mum on benefits in the space of two years, broke down. Obviously, her way of coping with all the problems she had was to not sit down and think about them, and we had just provided a space for her to do exactly what she had been avoiding. I was glad at that moment of my pastoral training, which helped us to bring things back to a manageable place for her before we left. Reflecting together in the car on the way home, I realised it had all been a bit of a shock for my tenants' association friend, who was not used to people he barely knew breaking down on him.

As we have rolled out Listen Up to other

areas, one thing in particular has really struck me. When people who are relatively affluent sit down and properly listen to people who are relatively poor, and vice versa, everyone leaves the encounter changed. Specific things that I have found happening include the following:

1   Both affluent and poor people may find themselves listened to and cared for in a way they have rarely experienced elsewhere (which can be very hard for both to handle).

2   Once you have seen and heard first-hand the poverty that people are living in, you can't 'un-see' it. You never see the world in quite the same way again. The look in affluent people's eyes coming away from these encounters is similar to the look you see in the eyes of a missionary who has lived in a completely different culture for some time.

3   The experience of being listened to properly, deeply and compassionately changes people. Immediately, they become a person, with a detailed story to tell, rather than a statistic, or someone to be judged by what can be seen on the surface.

As someone who is more affluent, Listen Up has created a distance between me and some of my fellow churchgoers. It's not the first time I have experienced this phenomenon. It probably began when I first started to go to St John's Park on the Wybourn all those years ago, in terms of how Christians from more affluent churches seemed to regard my situation. Just as a missionary from overseas sees things that they find it hard to convey to those back home, so I find it increasingly difficult to live with the apparent contradiction between what we preach, pray, read and sing about in church services and how involved we choose to be with those who are destitute on our doorstep. A sense of anger at the injustice of the situation has grown in me, but I am not sure that most people in church really care. I often find that we in the church are the slowest to listen and to show compassion, rather than the fastest, as I would have hoped, given the example of the life of Jesus.

But then I remember how I was, before I had these extraordinary encounters. How I knew poverty was there, but felt scared to get directly involved and be friends with anyone who was poorer. There's the fear that you will be overwhelmed by people's needs, and then there's the even greater fear that people might actually love you. Then what do you do? What do you do when someone who is from a totally different background, who has no money, turns out to have more genuine compassion for you than some of your family and friends, and certainly than your friends at church?

Lesley's story
(and part of the story of Murston Community Bank and Drop-in)

Lesley Jones is an assistant curate licensed to four parishes in Canterbury Diocese, including All Saints' Murston, an Urban Priority Area. Her community work spans three decades, including 'One for the Basket', an emergency food parcel network in Sunderland. Today Lesley co-ordinates a community project in Murston church.

Friends may say that I am a long way from home, which is in Durham. I am now in Kent and have adjusted quickly to life in Murston, near Sittingbourne. This may be partly due to the familiar socio-economic climate in areas like Murston, where many individual stories echo those of communities across the North East of England. During the initial visit to Murston church, someone had a quiet word in my ear: 'You do know that unemployment is very high around here ... and there are only a couple of people in the congregation that are in

work?' I'm afraid my response was sort of 'and?'
It didn't matter, it was neither off-putting nor
a challenge, the congregation simply reflect
this particular community. I began to wonder
what the individual stories were, and how they
related to the local church.

Murston – then and now

People are happy to share the story of
Murston. This is a community that grew as
a result of the brick-making industry in the
nineteenth century. 'Murston' bricks can be
found in famous landmarks across London.
More recently, despite many flourishing local
businesses, people have experienced a decline
in job opportunities. By 2013, conversation
after conversation described a neighbourhood
where many were finding it increasingly
difficult to make ends meet. As the recession
dragged on, families had fewer resources
available. People were living on or near the
breadline. The moneylenders were the ones
who were benefiting. Some of the people we
spoke to were at a point where they could no
longer access pay-day loans, even with interest
rates of 4,000 per cent, as their credit rating
was so poor. Others were relying on doorstep
lenders and paying huge levels of interest
for years to come, and there was evidence of

illegal money lending.[7] Listening to the day-to-day reality of frustration, embarrassment, pain, and for some a real sense of losing their dignity, we felt it important to do something as a church. We wanted to find a way of letting people know that the church cares about what was going on in their lives; the church cares because God cares.

Like many churches, All Saints Murston had set up different projects for the past 30 years or so, providing a range of services to the community. We began to ask if there was anything else that could be done to help families facing economic hardship and financial exclusion. We were already in a position to make referrals for food parcels. Could we further develop partnerships to help tackle some of the things that had led to the lack of food in the first place? Increasingly for me, food parcels became a sticking plaster on a gaping wound – and something more needed to be done.

Working in partnership

The difficulties around poverty are so devastating and widespread in many of our

[7] To find out if loan sharks are operating in your area, contact the National Illegal Money Lending Team on 0300 5552222 or email reportaloanshark@stoploansharks.gov.uk.

communities across the UK that no single organisation can begin to tackle this on its own. Working with others in partnership, sharing a common compassion for our neighbours, proved to be a way forward for us. Within our region a conversation began between the diocese and a local credit union, encouraging us to reflect where we were as a church; and encouraging us to discern where God could be in our response to the needs of the community.

A way in which we could move forward began to emerge. We had a whole host of people telling us they needed help with money and debt problems which were connected to other issues. We discovered an amazing skill set among our congregation, including two experienced bank personnel, administrators, tea-makers, pastoral listeners, and carpenters. We had a small congregation with little financial resource, but with people available on weekdays. There was an open invitation to explore what could be possible with the local credit union. The dots joined up and the church gave their blessing to open a branch of Kent Savers Credit Union in Murston church. This would be something totally beyond our collective experience, and that of Kent Savers, as it would be their very first branch. We received practical support from the diocese with a grant of £1,000 to get started. By the time we were ready to open the doors we had received training from the credit union and over £4,000 in either cash or kind from local authorities, churches, community groups and a local business. Working with our new partners including the Citizens Advice Bureau (CAB), the local Borough Council, the Community Safety Partnership, Kent Fire and Rescue Service, local schools and children's centres enabled us collectively to offer support on a broader range of issues.

We were now in a position to talk more widely as we continued to consult with our neighbours. It was as if we were saying 'It is okay to talk to us about anything – including money.' People responded by talking openly about issues of debt, domestic violence and other problems. Meeting followed meeting, and there was a great level of enthusiasm. Our aim as a church was to open in January 2014 – a time when across the country we begin to count the cost of Christmas celebrations, and most of us feel the pinch.

With support from the different sectors, local businesses and our devoted team of volunteers, things began to fall into place. We came up with a name for our branch, created necessary systems, accessed additional training, safeguarding, even designing our own pass books. There was also the physical transformation of part of the church building into a cafe-style space and credit union branch. In January 2014 the Bishop of Dover and Mayor of Swale officially opened Murston Community Bank,[8] alongside our neighbours from across the community. In the first few weeks we settled into a regular routine of opening the community bank Monday to Friday 10 a.m. until 12 noon. As part of our welcome and hospitality there were free hot drinks in our new cafe area. As we are not specialists in debt advice, the CAB provided a member of staff on Monday mornings to assist with anything from debt to employment issues and made referrals to other agencies through the week.

We usually pray before we open the doors, and again after each session, to remind us that we are engaging in this activity as Christians seeking to live out our Christian faith and care for others. We welcome people of all faiths and none, we are not there to judge but to accept people where they are, and through a combination of services on site and off, we have walked alongside many people in their hour of need.

---

[8] Follow us on Facebook at https://www.facebook.com/ Murston CommunityBank.

A loan is not always the answer

Although the credit union offers loans from a minimum of six months and a variety of rates from 5.9 per cent,[9] we soon discovered that due to levels of debt already incurred, another loan was sometimes the last thing that people needed. Often the loan request was for something very basic, essential or very short term while waiting for benefit payments. For example:

- a couple with a young family and only a microwave to heat food
- a partner off sick from work – managing to pay the bills but no money for food or heat
- the impact of the 'bedroom tax' taking its toll
- a family not already in receipt of benefits preventing access to crisis help when things went wrong
- a job appearing to be full-time but turning out to be for only one day a week
- too much money going out and not enough coming in.

The CAB were amazing when it came to helping people to dig themselves out of debt and having

---

[9] Interest rates correct, July 2014.

a base in Murston made a real difference too. If they could advise how to reduce outgoings and bring debt under control, then in the longer term there was no need for people to take out another loan. If we were able to access white goods, pass on something already donated to the church, such as a cooker, refrigerator or washing machine, there was no need to take out another loan. As each day passed we began to realise that what we had opened was more than a credit union branch – it was a community hub. We could provide someone financially excluded with a savings account, as well as access to support.

Our list of partners grew to include our Police Community Safety Officer and the Social Responsibility representatives at the local Job Centre. We began to work across partnerships to enable the CAB to offer a money-awareness course on behalf of the Job Centre in our church. We also hosted a Job Centre open day where residents could directly access different partners, such as housing associations and voluntary groups, as well as catch up with their advisor from the Job Centre. Feedback from this was very positive. The peaceful environment of the church building contributed to helpful conversations. The church was becoming the heart of the community, a place for the community, supporting others.

The project has been open just over six months now, and in that time we have seen dignity restored to individuals and situations. We have seen people return later seeking prayer or wanting to give something back to the church in terms of volunteer time. From the very beginning we have had more contact with people who would not consider themselves regular churchgoers. We understand their time spent in Murston Community Bank and Drop-in has had a positive impact on their lives. It is really wonderful when we can create a space for someone to volunteer, see their confidence grow, and have to find a replacement when they find a full-time job. What we have done is create an inclusive space, within a church, where people can come together, using the little resources we have, and working in partnership with others. If you are lonely there is someone to talk to; if you need urgent help you can find it; if you want to save and open a Christmas account you can do that; and if a loan is the way forward for you, then we can assist with the paperwork.

By listening carefully to the stories of Murston and not turning away from the hardships people faced, the church has refreshed its approach to mission and learning. By making time to reflect together on our experiences in the light of the gospel messages, we are deepening our discipleship and beginning to see growth, spiritually and numerically, particularly in the area of baptisms. Visitors to the drop-in and community bank often join us for Messy Church, while others are finding their way to other church events. We are still a relatively small congregation, with few people in work, but we have found a way in which we can understand church as the body of Christ in a very practical way, where all are valued, all have a role and a sense of purpose – church as a place where we all can grow in faith, together.

So when it comes to an inclusive church, I think our message is this:

- Listen to your community and pray together.
- Place the love of God at the heart of your response.
- Remember everyone is welcome.
- Work with others in partnership.

PART 2

Theology

Bread for the Whole Body: A Theology of Poverty for an Inclusive Church
SUSAN DURBER

Each book in this series contains a substantial theological reflection by an expert in the field. Here Susan Durber helps us reflect on how we may be a church not for the poor but of the poor.

SUSAN DURBER is a minister of the United Reformed Church and has served pastorates in Manchester, Salford and Oxford. Until 2013 she was Principal of Westminster College in Cambridge, and now works for Christian Aid as Theology Advisor. She serves on the Faith and Order Commission of the World Council of Churches. Her most recent book is *Surprised by Grace: Parables and prayers* (2013), published by the United Reformed Church.

Introduction

If the poor are not included within the church, that may or may not always be experienced as a problem for 'the poor', but it will always be a problem for the church. If the church becomes enslaved to a particular set of social groups or exclusively to those who are powerful, and forgets its basic calling to be 'the body of Christ', then it will cease to be the church. Again and again, in the Gospels, we discover a Christ who tells us that it is the poor who are blessed, the poor who know their need of God and that it is with the poor that we will find him. A church without those who know their need of God makes no sense at all! So this question about whether the church is inclusive of 'the poor' is a fundamental and crucial one.

But what does it mean to be poor? Who are 'the poor'? It might be tempting to define poverty solely in terms of financial resources. There is one kind of definition of poverty which says that the world's poor are those who live on less than US$1.25 a day. Few people in Britain live in that kind of condition of absolute poverty. But Christian Aid, for example, defines poverty much more broadly as:

> a lack of power; the power for example, to have your say and be heard, or to know your rights and demand them; the power to have access to essential services or to share fairly in the world's resources or to live in the security not only of surviving, but also of thriving.[10]

This kind of definition helps us to see poverty in a more holistic way, as something that we recognise as a reality in the lives of people in countries like Britain, as well as in parts of the world where there is extreme food poverty. It helps us to recognise that poverty is something that is about exclusion from society, culture and human community, and that it might also be about exclusion from the faith community. A definition like that also helps us to know that poverty is not always so easy to 'see' around us and that it is not always as obvious as we might suppose.

[10] *Partnership for Change, Executive Summary*, Christian Aid, 2012, p. 3.

CHAPTER 1

A church without the poor

Historical background

There is a prevalent perception that the church in Britain is largely a middle-class institution, and that churchgoers are largely not 'poor', but generally have good access to resources, education, social power and security of life. And, although it may not be quite so straightforward and simple as that, this perception is grounded in a measure of truth. Historians will tell us that when the Industrial Revolution came in the early nineteenth century and large parts of the population moved to, or grew within, the new urban areas, they never made a connection with the church there. Perhaps they were leaving behind patterns of churchgoing and attendance associated with near feudal allegiances in the countryside. Perhaps the churches in urban settings seemed different and alien from the country parishes they had known. Perhaps they were simply glad not to feel obliged to go any more. The new industrialists built churches for their workers and the established churches built new parish churches, but much of the evidence suggests that these new, often ambitiously large, churches and chapels were never full. The 1851 census revealed what many were shocked to discover, that many people in the new industrialised world of Victorian Britain did not go to church. Churchgoing became within this new world, in some ways, a signifier of respectability and improvement. Churches came to be associated with movements like the Temperance Movement, and with movements for education and political and social change. Churches of many kinds became agents of social transformation for their members. The new urban poor were more often the recipients of the charity of churches than members of those churches, though there were exceptions.

It was certainly true that, rather earlier than many would suspect, there was a profound change in British culture. No longer did 'everyone' attend church, but some people 'chose' to attend church and which church to attend. Church was no longer something that 'included' everyone as part of a unified culture, but became, like many other institutions, part of a complex world in which social class was variously signified.

You cannot read a Victorian novel without realising that Dissenters did not have as high a social standing as 'church folk', for example, and that, generally speaking, the 'poor', and especially the urban poor, did not go to church at all. The British landscape is peppered with church buildings which evoke this world. In a class-dominated culture, the church became largely class defined too. And in churches which reflected more and more the values of those of the growing middle classes, so they came to 'exclude' those who were poor. In a church of 'Sunday best', of voluntary financial giving, of pew rents, of Sunday 'school' and improvement, even if no one meant to, the poor were excluded. And as church came to be associated with being charitable and improving the lot of the poorest of society, so it became an institution which acted *towards* the poor, but in which they were not themselves included. Many in churches today still mourn the lost days of vast 'Sunday schools' (particularly the annual outings), of sales of work and annual walks, quoting the large numbers that filled the church or school room on such occasions. But the truth is, sadly, that those vast numbers of people saw themselves as the recipients of the church's (good) work, and not always as its members. There were many good and faithful attempts, both from the centre and at the fringes of the churches, to create church movements or services which would indeed 'bring in' the poor, but still the church became, despite itself, a church which did not include the poor but rather acted towards them.

The church in the UK today

However, the situation today, in twenty-first-century Britain, is rather more varied than this historical analysis suggests. It remains true that many of the long-established churches still reflect the deeply embedded and familiar class lines of British culture. You can still find villages where the accents at the parish church are different from those at the Nonconformist chapel. You can still find churches in Urban Priority Areas where a faithful few, who have often travelled in from elsewhere, meet in a vast church to which the surrounding population never come. You can still find smart congregations in the suburbs and you can find a new metropolitan urban elite gathering for church in ways that affirm today's aspiring and ambitious middle classes. You can still find forms of church that mirror the social structure of contemporary culture and that therefore, even unwittingly, exclude people.

You can also find now, particularly in large urban settings, churches that have their origins in contexts other than Britain, which are often largely made up of migrant populations, who have brought their own styles and forms of church with them. These churches often reflect contexts in which the church certainly does not reflect the class divisions of Britain, but which will often be very much a church *of* the poor. In our largest cities, many Christian worshippers now will be black and minority ethnic (BME), sometimes but not always of first- or second-generation migrants, who will belong to communities where church is still for 'everyone' in many ways: for the whole family of all ages, for those who are wealthy and secure and those who are struggling financially. They may be defined along lines of language or culture, but they are often churches which do include those in poverty. As British church life reflects the changing face of Britain, so the story of the church's relationship to the poor also changes.

The Roman Catholic Church might also be considered another kind of exception to the British churches' story in relation to the poor. For centuries, Roman Catholics in Britain have been themselves marginalised from mainstream culture, whether or not they were wealthy or poor. But in recent years social prejudice against Catholics in Britain has been considerably overcome and migration from an extended European community, among other factors, has meant that numbers of worshippers have considerably increased. But the Roman Catholic Church, partly at least because of its real identity as a global church, a truly world community, has had a very different relationship to poverty from churches in Britain which have had a more national or local sense of their context. It is a church that has also managed, in many places, to be a church that, while it has served the poor, has also included them among its core community.

Hidden poverty in the church

In some contexts and congregations it may be the case that those living in poverty (however defined) are indeed sometimes present in our churches in Britain, but their poverty is rendered invisible because the church has a predominantly middle-class culture and practice. This culture often includes a particular kind of silence about the things that would enable poverty to be identified, discussed or addressed. It is striking that, often in church life, questions about money, giving and resources are surrounded by such confidentiality and silence that it might be impossible to know who in a congregation might be poor. There sometimes seems to be a stronger taboo about money and personal wealth than almost anything else! This makes the Iona Community's expectations that its members will open up their financial situation to the scrutiny and advice of others really remarkable. This silence means that members of a church congregation who have less money might simply be unable to participate in some parts of church life (the annual retreat or church outing), and might feel embarrassed, disempowered and excluded from the, often frequent, requests to give money, whether to church funds or to development charities. Many of those who administer church funds will testify that it is often the poorest people (on fixed or low incomes) who will be the most generous givers, but it is hard to deny that if you are living on very limited resources, then it can be a challenge to feel that you truly belong to the church community.

It would certainly not be true to say that there are no churches in Britain where someone in poverty would be welcome or would feel at home. Churches are enormously varied and it is hard, if not foolish, to make generalisations. But there is a sense that, since the Industrial Revolution in Britain, the churches have ceased to be inclusive places where everyone belongs, but have been 'captured' by a complex class culture. While those churches which have side-stepped this aspect of British culture, because their roots are elsewhere, have a different relationship with people in poverty, what we sometimes still call the mainstream churches have largely come to be identified as middle class. This is not a deliberate exclusion of those who are poor, but it is a real one. The British church, in many of its forms, has become a church without the poor, and very often good people are left asking themselves 'Why?'

Theology in a church 'without the poor'?

What does this reflection on the British church context suggest for a theology of poverty? It is striking, though not the least surprising, that churches which are 'churches without the poor' will reflect theologically about poverty in particular ways. Such reflection will often be done from a place of kindness but of distance, and not from the kind of knowledge which comes from experience of poverty or even from real solidarity with those who are poor. It might be a theology that finds it hard to engage with the Jesus who said that the poor were blessed, because it might persist in seeing 'the poor' as unfortunate victims waiting to be rescued. It will be theology from a distance, not forged in relationship and mutuality, and not shaped by experience from within the church community itself. It will, almost inevitably, be a theology which focuses on the significance of the response of 'the rich' or (as we often put it) the 'more fortunate' towards those in poverty, so that the theological reflection is focused on how, through kindness and generosity, those who have might steward their resources and develop their own virtue. In a church without 'the poor', theology will begin from the place and the experience of the rich. This may be true whether this is a local congregation or an entire denomination. At its very worst, of course, reflection on poverty from 'a church without the poor' might lead to the kind of theology echoed in that infamous Victorian hymn verse:

> The rich man in his castle,
> the poor man at his gate,
> God made them high and lowly,
> and ordered their estate.[11]

This is a theology of poverty which doesn't see

---

[11] Cecil Frances Alexander.

it as a scandal or as a question of justice, as a structural problem for us all which demands to be changed, or even as misfortune, but merely as the 'ways things are', as set by God. And it is a kind of theology which might even relieve the rich of the need to cultivate virtue, kindness and generosity! It takes a feat of imagination now to see how this understanding could have found willing supporters, but it is a kind of theology that gives comfort to the rich and that makes sense of the world to those who have much to gain from the status quo. It is not a theology that could be spoken from a church that truly included those in poverty. There would be too great a gulf from lived experience, and this kind of heresy would be exposed for the lie that it is.

A 'church without the poor', in a world in which poverty, inequality and suffering are real, is not only likely, almost inevitably, to have deeply distorted values, but it is also excluded from a source of knowledge. It is not only that its perspective is skewed, but that there are things it simply cannot know. It was Sandra Harding who suggested that those who are suffering, those 'for whom the shoe pinches' in this world, are those whose voices have what she calls a 'strong objectivity'.[12] They are a source of knowledge, and so without those voices in the church, a source of truth is missing. This is not simply about information, but about a way of knowing, even a way of knowing God. The church cannot really speak about what it doesn't know. The World Council of Churches has warned of a danger of 'the bourgeois captivity of theology'.[13] There are moments in the church's life and history when this has been all too evident. This is part of the theological damage that is done when a church does not truly include those in poverty.

[12] This phrase comes from her book *Whose Science? Whose Knowledge? Thinking from women's lives*, Ithaca, NY: Cornell University Press, 1991.

[13] *Towards a Church of Poor*, Geneva: World Council of Churches, 1979, p. 117.

CHAPTER 2

A church for the poor

A church strong in service

The church in Britain, even while it has often been a 'church without the poor', has often also been a church '*for* the poor'. The churches in Britain have often been strong and leading agents in responding to poverty in Britain and globally. There are many churches who would hardly know what to do if they were not engaged in alleviating poverty in some form or other. It is well known that churchgoers are more generous in giving to charities than some other sectors of society, and that they often make long-term commitments to change. The church has a strong culture of charitable giving. Many churches have projects which are addressing domestic poverty, from soup kitchens to food banks, from credit unions to drop-in centres, from homeless shelters to Christmas gifts to children. The churches in Britain also have an astonishing history of addressing global poverty, whether through projects which address direct humanitarian need or by supporting agencies like Christian Aid which seek to address the root causes of poverty and which have the ambition to overcome it. There are variations among churches about the level of activity and commitment to these projects, but there is absolutely no doubt that they are a key part of contemporary church life among an increasing variety of churches. Whether churches have traditionally seen themselves as committed to 'social justice', whether they are members of the Evangelical Alliance, whether they are independent or connexional, established or nonconformist, churches in Britain are well known, if for nothing else, than for trying to respond to urgent social needs and to give themselves in service. It is also church groups, above all, in Britain who can be readily encouraged to engage in advocacy and campaigning on issues of poverty. The Jubilee Debt campaign, the IF campaign and the Tax Justice campaigns of recent times bear testimony to this. Church communities also pray for those who are poor as a regular part of Sunday and often daily worship, and for many churches a gospel that did not include the promise of the feeding of the hungry and the setting free of the oppressed would hardly be the gospel at all. Many churches, of all kinds, are engaged in serving those who are poor, in alleviating poverty in different ways, in speaking up for the poor and in seeking to change the ways in which poverty might be ended.

A recent British TV documentary called *Benefits Street* was highly controversial. The people who lived in a street in the Winson Green area in Birmingham were subject to a 'fly on the wall' style of filming. Though it is hard, and would be foolish, to draw too many conclusions from a much criticised programme, it was interesting to see how churches featured. They were presented as deeply engaged in the community. One man from the street went to a workshop offering help with job applications, and another went seeking help from a food bank. The churches featured in *Benefits Street* were, truly impressively, *for* the poor. The people in the churches were clearly unfailingly gracious, generous and understanding, giving of their time and resources beyond expectations. But it seemed, as least from this programme, that the churches were mostly experienced by those who lived in 'the street' as places to go to for help, rather than as places to which you might belong.

The theology of a church 'for the poor'?

Many churches and agencies draw their theological understanding of what they are doing from the very heart of the gospel. Jesus came to announce the Kingdom of God, which was symbolised and indeed already brought into being at the tables at which he fed those who were hungry and gave everyone a seat, in a foretaste of the banquet of life for all. They draw from visionary and inspiring writers who have insisted that the church is *for* the poor, that its very purpose is to be 'on the side' of the poor, even to have a 'preferential option for the poor'.[14]

But, the problem is that unless the church can be the church *of* the poor as well as *for* the poor, it will never develop a theology that is adequate to the task of naming the truth about poverty or indeed of changing it. Despite its long history of sacrificial service in addressing poverty, the church has a more ready theology of *service* than it has a theology of *transformation*. Both of these are undoubtedly important parts of the Christian life of discipleship, and a church without either is lacking something from its heart. Without the voice of the poor being at the heart of the church's life as real contributors and participants, rather than as recipients of service, real and lasting change will not happen. Even though the churches work hard, even though they understand the addressing of poverty as vital to the gospel and to Jesus'

[14] A phrase which came from the churches in Latin America, and which has become an oft-quoted theme of what came to be known as liberation theology.

mission, death and resurrection, a church which is still a church *without* the poor will be itself impoverished and will not be resourced, empowered and inspired to transform poverty.

Sometimes the church, so devoted in service as it is, gives itself away when it reflects on its work for the poor. There have been stories of church communities being 'delighted' that there is a need in their town for a food bank because this gives the church an opportunity to serve the community. Local newspapers sometimes carry pictures of smiling church members ready to open a soup kitchen or food bank and celebrating their achievement in providing resources and volunteers. Of course this kind of emergency response to basic human need is Christ-like in its generosity. But if it is not accompanied by sorrow, anger even, that there is such human need in the first place and that it has been created by an unjust society, then it becomes distorted. The very existence of food banks should not be seen first as a sign of the church's generosity, but first as a sign of a sinful world. A church that is *for* the poor may well find itself rejoicing in the opportunity to serve, but a church that is *of* the poor, truly in solidarity with and made up of the poor, will 'see things differently' and will want to shout, protest and cry out as much as it gathers resources to feed hungry mouths.

Even those voices in the church who do a great deal to encourage the church to be, as it should be, a church *of* the poor sometimes find this hard to put into words in ways that do not exclude. Pope Francis, for example, in *Evangelii Gaudium*, says,

'We have to state, without mincing words, that there is an inseparable bond between our faith and the poor. May we never abandon them.'[15]

There is so much that is so very positive about this text, but who is the 'we' here and who are 'the poor'? It is not that they should not be abandoned by 'us', but that they should be part of the 'us'. Pope Francis shows every sign of believing this and living it out, but the church seems to find it very difficult to say, as Jesus did, 'Blessed are you who are poor', as though it is addressing those right in its midst, those who are part of it. There is then a continual temptation for the church to understand itself as 'other' than the poor, as servant of the poor rather than as community of the poor. This means that it is sometimes beguiled by a theology of diakonia, a theology of service, as its primary response to poverty, rather than a theology of solidarity,

15 *Evangelii Gaudium*, London: Catholic Truth Society, 2013, p. 29.

or a theology of communion of rich and poor together, or a theology that hopes and works for a real transformation of the world. If the church is truly to be the community of Christ, the very body of Christ, then it needs to include within its centre those who are poor, so that the world may be transformed. A church that is defined only in terms of being a church *for* the poor will not be true to its real mission and nature.

Sam Wells, the Vicar of St Martin-in-the-Fields in Trafalgar Sqaure, in his lecture 'What's Wrong with Poverty',[16] has argued that the addressing of poverty is not best understood as being about the overcoming of someone else's limitations, but is about overcoming isolation, about communion. He urges the church not to think of itself as being *for* other people, but about being *with* them, just as God is not only on our side, but came to be *with* us in the incarnation of God's Son. Perhaps Sam Wells' insight could be seen as a very necessary first step in addressing poverty rather than the only step (to be 'with' in the best sense might lead on to seeking redress of the injustice that is then truly experienced), but his insight is surely crucial. The problem is not simply that the church has misunderstood poverty, but that

---

[16] Delivered at St Mary-le-Bow Church in London, 19 March 2014.

the only way really to understand what poverty is must be to find that out *with* those who are poor themselves. The way to knowledge, the way to the understanding that we need here, is not simply the kind of knowledge that can be gleaned at a distance, but is the kind that can only truly be found by getting as close up as human beings can be – in the intimate, often challenging, place of human interaction, in the place where the world may need to change, fundamentally. Being *with* is the place to begin and the place to linger until there is no longer the kind of distinction between *us* and *them* that can be sustained, but only really us. When we are truly *with* then the structures already begin to change.

This need to be more than *for* the poor is as much about global poverty as it is about domestic poverty. It may be easier, in a physical sense, to be close to the homeless and hungry in Britain, but it is no less important to be *with* those in poverty in contexts very different from our own. Of course not everyone can do this literally (and the pace of climate change would be quickened if we tried), but it is also important that we sense the significance of solidarity, and the impact it has on 'our' desire to change things about the world and ourselves, in relation to 'the poor' everywhere.

It is important that relationships do not foster the kind of dependency that gives 'us' a kind of satisfaction, but that are ultimately demeaning for others. It is vital that, in terms of church relationships, we really discover our communion and solidarity across miles and traditions, and that we address poverty from that place together. The life of the church in the global North is profoundly impoverished if it does not share in the theological insights in which churches of the global South are rich. The expectation of being *for* others will often drive us to want to provide others with what we ourselves desire or have had, and there is no listening and learning from the wisdom which others have found and which could enrich us.

The church in Britain has a long, and in so many ways admirable, tradition and experience of being *for* the poor. In some periods of our history it has been the voice of the church above all that has spoken out for justice and inspired people to address poverty.[17] In periods when governments and governing classes have preferred to abandon those with little or even preferred to create newly excluded groups, it has often been the church which has addressed need, spoken up and faced ridicule for doing so.

[17] The publication of the *Faith in the City* report during Margaret Thatcher's time in government is one example.

There is no doubt that the church, and often at its best, has been *for* the poor. Christian faith has inspired and enacted mercy and compassion in many sacrificial and heroic ways. But even this generous and, sometimes prophetic, work has been less faithful, truthful and transformative than it could have been because that church has not been always *with* the poor, and those in poverty have not always been at home or part of the community of the church.

Dorothee Soelle, a theologian who might justifiably be described as the liberation theologian of Europe, once wrote that 'A theology which does not articulate the suffering community, does not speak from it, think from it, feel from it, is de facto a theology of oppression.'[18]

The church in Britain has long spoken *for* the poor, often with a prophetic and brave voice, but Soelle's trenchant voice suggests that if the church does not speak *from* the poor, then it continues to speak a theology of oppression. These are shocking and disturbing words, but there is profound truth here. A church that is *for* the poor, but not *of* the poor, is still a church which cannot speak authentically of the gospel.

---

[18] Dorothee Soelle, *Thinking about God: An introduction to theology*, London: SCM Press, 1990, p. 97.

CHAPTER 3

A church of the poor

A very different church with a renewed theology

When the church does include the poor, and when those who are living with poverty are shaping the church's life, its discourse, its habits and practice, then something unmistakeable happens and everything is different. Of course there have been and there are churches which have had those in poverty in the pews and in their communities, but without *really* including their experience, their concerns, their hopes and their understanding of God. But in some places, where those in poverty are truly included, the church itself is changed.

In some communities what is immediately challenged is a sentimentalising of poverty that sometimes characterises parts of the church. Those who know about the poverty which is about a lack of power, of basic resources and rights, a denial of a voice and of basic freedoms, know that this is not the same as taking a 'vow of poverty' as freely chosen, or making a commitment to live a life of simplicity, letting go of the burden of possessions. Vows and commitments like that are taken out of a place of power to choose, and though taking them is a significant and holy commitment, they are not the same as the experience of poverty which far too many in our world suffer. Gustavo Gutiérrez, the theologian who might be justly called the father of Liberation theology, describes poverty thus:

> In the final analysis, poverty means death: lack of food and housing, the inability to attend properly to health and education needs, the exploitation of workers, permanent unemployment, the lack of respect for one's human dignity, and unjust limitations placed on personal freedom in the areas of self-expression, politics, and religion. Poverty is a situation that destroys peoples, families, and individuals ... [it is] 'institutionalised violence'[19]

This is an understanding of poverty that comes from a church *of* the poor. It is an understanding

[19] Gustavo Gutiérrez, *A Theology of Liberation*, revised edition with a new Preface, Maryknoll, NY: Orbis Books, 1988, p. xxi.

that does not glamorous or romanticise it, but
sees it for what it is, a kind of violence and a
kind of death. He also affirms that

> it is important to realize that being
> poor is a way of living, thinking,
> loving, praying, believing and hoping,
> spending leisure time, and struggling
> for a livelihood. Being poor today is
> also increasingly coming to mean being
> involved in the struggle for justice and
> peace, defending one's life and freedom,
> seeking a more democratic participation
> in the decisions made by society ... and
> being committed to the liberation of
> every human being.[20]

Gutiérrez might also be accused of romanticism
here, in a context where gang cultures and crime
are rife, where domestic violence is endemic
and where often those in poverty are simply
struggling to survive, but he does reflect well the
ways in which those who are poor do not want
'handouts' or 'aid' in the classic sense. What are
needed are radical changes to the structure of
societies and cultures, such that those who are
in poverty can be empowered to lift themselves

---

[20] Gutiérrez, *A Theology of Liberation*, p. xxii.

out of poverty. This is why agencies like Christian Aid work so hard on the root causes of poverty, on empowering people, and on changing governments, laws and fiscal arrangements.

A church which truly includes those in poverty, and in which their voice is heard, will be a very different one from the church which is without them, or even simply *for* them. There is something about the urgency of what is seen as the scandal and 'death' of poverty that demands a much more radical kind of response than the kind of service that responds to immediate need. A church of the poor will understand Gutiérrez's sense that poverty is 'death' and that the Christian theological response to 'death' must be not burial, or even anointing, but rather resurrection, a change so radical that death itself (poverty itself) is defeated. A response to poverty is not then seen as a kind of consequence of the gospel in the sense of good works in response to grace, but as the heart of the gospel itself. A church really experiencing the scandal, pain and terror of poverty at its heart simply could not resign itself to poverty as an inevitable part of life and could not take the words of Jesus, 'you will have the poor with you always' at face value. It could not even settle for sustained compassion, and for poverty and its ameliorating as a constant of church and human life. It could not settle for 'help', for pity and kindness, when it becomes so evident that it is justice that is required! A church truly of the poor would demand that poverty should be *ended*, and would see that hope as close to the heart of the gospel message itself. It could not spiritualise salvation, but would see the end of poverty as, in part at least, what salvation truly is. It would have a theology that would speak to the daily needs of all the people in a way that is as bodily, real and vital as the pain of poverty. It would be a church that could never accept that poverty could be acceptable, at any level, either to God or to the church, and it would be committed to giving attention to the poor and their needs, just as Jesus himself was.

One very powerful example of how it makes a difference to be a church *of* the poor is the collection of transcripts of Bible studies conducted in the community of Solentiname in Nicaragua[21]. Here, in these insights into a method of reflection, along with the fruits of that study done in a new context, is evidence of how the reading of scripture is transformed in a church of the poor. The *campesinos* of Solentiname reveal insights into Bible

[21]   Ernesto Cardenal, *The Gospel of Solentiname*, Maryknoll, NY: Orbis Books, 2010.

stories, many of them once told in peasant communities like their own, which biblical scholars from a church ensnared by its own wealth have missed for centuries. They do not 'spiritualise' stories, but see in stories about economics and power, poverty and empire, the realities of their own lives and the hope for the ways in which God is transforming them. This little collection of transcripts has proved revolutionary in opening up new ways of engaging with the scriptures, and has been received by and influenced churches very far from its beginnings in Nicaragua. The church, in many places, has come to understand the kind of distorting lies which have become the norm among churches from whom those in poverty have been, for whatever reason, excluded. This exclusion has affected even the way in which we have read the Bible, the first source of our theology. And this is now beginning to change. This little book and the story of its reception reveals so powerfully how a church *of* is a different place.

Pope Francis, in his apostolic exhortation *Evangelii Gaudium*, writes compellingly about the inclusion of the poor within society, and within the church. He argues that it is the ministry of Christ, who himself became poor, and who was always close to the poor, which provides the basis for this concern. He writes about the need for the church to hear the 'cry for justice' of the poor, to work to eliminate the structural causes of poverty, and to live in solidarity which he defines as 'a new mindset which thinks in terms of community and the priority of life of all over the appropriation of goods by a few'.[22]

But his writing on this subject comes not from an outsider's perspective, but from living in close relationship with those who are poor. He refers, for example, to the work of the bishops of Brazil, who, speaking from the experience of poverty in Brazil, protest about its scandal and injustice. Pope Francis also writes movingly about what he calls 'the special place of the poor in God's people'; God became incarnate in poverty and the history of redemption takes place among the poor, from the 'yes' of a young woman in a town on the edge of empire to Jesus' declaration of his message as being good news for the poor. He says that those who are poor share in the faith, but they also know, better than others, the suffering of Christ. He says that we need to be evangelised by the poor. He writes:

---

[22] *Evangelii Gaudium*, London: Catholic Truth Society, 2013, p. 95.

The new evangelization is an invitation to acknowledge the saving power at work in their lives and to put them at the centre of the Church's pilgrim way. We are called to find Christ in them, to lend our voice to their causes, but also to be their friends, to listen to them, to speak for them and to embrace the mysterious wisdom which God wishes to share with us through them.[23]

He says that he is not talking about programmes of assistance (aid and service or works of mercy and charity) but the kind of attentiveness which is based on a being 'at one' with those in poverty. For Pope Francis, this is also not only so that we can, as a church, better understand poverty and respond to it profoundly in order to end it, but this is about understanding and even receiving God. It is a theological imperative.

Only on the basis of this real and sincere closeness can we properly accompany the poor on their path of liberation. Only this will ensure that 'in every Christian community the poor feel at home. Would

[23] *Evangelii Gaudium*, p. 100.

not this approach be the greatest and
most effective presentation of the good
news of the kingdom?'[24]

And Pope Francis makes it clear that everyone
in the Christian community should make it
their business to be 'close to the poor'; no one
should be exempt from this and from a concern
for social justice. He writes passionately about
the dangers of an increasingly individualistic
society in which we are cut off from each other
and from each other's realities and experiences,
and he reiterates the concern from Catholic
social teaching that we should give ourselves
for the 'common good'.

While sometimes the style of writing, and
the difficulties of expression, mean that 'the
poor' seem, in this exhortation, to be contrasted
with 'we', it is clear that Pope Francis absolutely
believes that the church, if it is true to itself as
church, is a church *of* the poor, and that it must
be a community in which those in poverty are
included. For him this is for theological as well
as justice reasons, since Christ himself was
incarnate among and with those in poverty. In
his writing it is very evident that the church
cannot be the church if the poor are excluded. At

[24] *Evangelii Gaudium*, pp. 100–1 – and here Pope Francis is
quoting John Paul II.

the same time, he does not romanticise 'the poor' in the sense of believing that poverty should not be changed. On the contrary, the presence of the poor in the church serves to light in us a fire of protest about the scandal of poverty and urges upon us the real demands for social justice. Pope Francis comes, of course, from Argentina and he shares in the Latin American traditions which see salvation not as something solely 'spiritual', but as embracing the whole of human life. He sees the dignity in those who are poor, and he believes that they are God's evangelists, having knowledge and truth which others need to hear and discover, but he also wants justice to come and poverty to be ended.

In so many ways, the church is called to be a church *of* the poor and not one that either excludes them or only acts towards them (even if such action is inspired by the deepest kindness and love). In order for the church to be the church it must be a community in which those who live in poverty are present, are heard, are even regarded as particularly close to God. Then the church cannot help but respond to the scandal of poverty, because it feels it within its very body. And then the church also hears the gospel, which is carried and embodied in those who are living in poverty, just as Christ himself was incarnate in poverty.

CHAPTER 4

A church which is giving and recieving

The church as a community sharing bread around one table

All of this reflection is moving towards a sense that the church is called to be a community in which humanity meets itself and in which the realities of life are discovered not in abstract but through relationship with people, and this must be a central insight for an inclusive church. The communion table, the place where the body of Christ gathers and where the body of Christ is received, is a place at which all the people of God meet each other and meet with God on an equal footing. The communion table cannot be the place where only some can gather; it is the place to which Christ calls all of us. And at the heart of the Christian faith is the understanding that we are who we are in communion with others. This means that our relating to one another cannot be about a kind of instrumentality, as though we are only here to 'do' certain things 'for' one another.

The Christian life is not about co-operation for a common cause, even the most worthy one, it is about communion and community. This means that in a church 'without the poor' communion is broken and the church is not being the church.

A church in which we know our dependence on God and on each other

A key insight that such a sense of communion gives us is that we are all of us, whoever we are, dependent on the free gift of God. When we are together, at the communion table, we see that some of the default ways in which we understand who we are and how we stand in the world are simply false. For much of our lives we, or at least those who are wealthy, place a high value on human power and initiative, on our own 'rights' and our own abilities to determine our lives. But at the communion table, or on our knees before God, we see that we are first of all dependent upon God's grace, and upon one another. We discover that there is more to life, more to reality, than what I can control and determine, that there is something wonderfully 'gift-like' about the life I have and lead. We learn to receive with thankfulness and to recognise our dependence on others, and on God. We recognise that we do not 'own' things, life, love, and much more, in the way that we usually assume we do. And then we recognise that this being dependent, being recipients of God's gift of life, is not limiting, but freeing. Those who live in poverty often know this before us and we share with them a need to learn to receive. At the heart of the church we discover that the human community is not made up of some who are dependent and some who are free, but that all are dependent and all may be free. It somehow breaks down the divide between what we like to call the 'haves and the have nots', and reveals something profound about what it means to be human. The illusion that riches can bring (that you can control your own future) is shown to be just that, and our mutual need for giving and receiving is revealed.

A healthy church community is one in which all know their need of God and of each other, and in which all give of themselves to give to others. In such a church, the divide between rich and poor begins to break down as everyone begins to see that all may be poor in some things and all may be rich in others. This is not then another way of sentimentalising poverty (in which the poor just turn out to be rich in 'other' things and are not really poor after all!), but a way of recognising our mutual poverty, and our mutual strength in responding to poverty together. It is a way of recognising, for the rich, that the world does not belong to 'us', that each person has both needs and something to contribute, and that everyone has gifts which others will welcome and which others cannot do without. It also moves us from a place in which the 'rich' are encouraged to be 'generous' with what belongs to them and to 'give' to those who are poor, to a place in which we recognise that there is a sense in which none of us 'own' anything, and in which our role is to make sure that all may receive the most generous gifts of life, and that what any of us 'owns' is not ours to keep if others are suffering.

We are who we are because of each other, in relationship

A theology of poverty needs to begin, then, not with a political or economic analysis of poverty (though that should certainly not be ignored), but with an exploration of human relationship. If we believe that all human beings are made in the image of God, then we cannot expect to understand who God is without relationship with others, and with all others. As Rowan Williams has put it:

> Central to what Christian theology sets before us is mutuality ... The model of human existence which is taken for granted is one in which each person is both needy and needed, both dependent

on others and endowed with gifts for others ... Jesus' own teaching and practice make it quite explicit that the renewed people of God cannot exist when certain categories are systematically excluded, so that the wholeness of the community requires them to be invited.[25]

He argues that if we take it for granted that my own well-being is inseparable from the well-being of all others, then we cannot settle for a world in which some will always continue to be poor. Our community with, our oneness with, those in poverty will itself impel us to end poverty. And this is not simply because we feel an imperative to 'be generous', but because we recognise our own oneness with, and even dependence upon, those who might seem to have nothing. Our 'destiny', as Rowan Williams puts it, is connected with the poor of the world, and of course the poor who live just around the corner. This is why a theology of poverty has to begin with this sense of relationship, and this is why the church needs to be a community which includes the poor, indeed why it cannot really be the church without doing so.

This beginning in the place of relationship

---

[25] Rowan Williams, 'Theology and Economics' in *Faith in the Public Square*, London: Bloomsbury, 2012, p. 228.

will also keep us from what has sometimes become a rather instrumental and limited sense of what 'justice' is. Sometimes we can be tempted to think of justice as being about what is 'owed' to a person, particularly of course ourselves. But justice, in the biblical traditions, is far more than something about redistribution or fairness, more than something that could be viewed almost like a kind of arithmetic; two for you and two for me. 'Doing justice', in the sense in which the prophet Micah speaks about it, is more than this. It is about being in a relationship such that you want to make sure that the 'other' has what is 'right' for them. It is about love and mercy too, about the kind of response to another human being that is rooted in a sense of your common humanity and interdependence.

A church then which includes those who are poor will be one in which poverty and wealth are understood very differently from those ways which focus on ownership or rights. It will be a church that cares so deeply about all its people, and indeed the people of the world around it, that poverty will be intolerable and passion for change will be deep. It will be one in which everyone understands that they are poor and rich together and that the world they share needs to be changed.

CHAPTER 5

A church to end poverty

The inclusion of those in poverty within the life of the church will certainly not mean that the church will accept that poverty should continue; far from it! The inclusion of 'the poor' is not simply about including another category of people within a diverse community, about 'accepting people as they are', but it is about changing the church and the world. This kind of inclusion does not simply shift the boundary of church, but it changes the church's life for good, and indeed makes it more possible for it to be the church.

There are many other kinds of inclusion which are founded on the promise and hope that people are accepted with no expectation of change. But the inclusion of those in poverty is rather different from this. The inclusion of those in poverty within the church will mean that everyone, and everything, should change. The church is much more radically equipped and empowered to end poverty. Its scandal can no longer be ignored, the 'violence' of poverty will be experienced by the whole church, and the insights of the poor will be embraced. The gospel itself will be understood more clearly, as everyone sees that the Christ who became poor is the one who reaches out to all to transform the world and to set the oppressed free. A church of the poor will want to end poverty and will give its life to that. It will also want to embrace another kind of poverty, a simplicity of life, a new relationship to creation and a true and deepening sense of dependence on God, because it will recognise that the ways of life that make many 'rich' are also those that leave others 'poor'.

Reflection on a story of Jesus: crossing the divide
The parable of the rich man and Lazarus: Luke 16:19–31

In Jesus' own teaching there is continued reflection about riches and poverty. In a culture where people thought that riches were a sign of blessing from God, he told people that it was the poor who were blessed. He told one rich man to sell everything that he possessed, and in that short instruction revealed to the man what his real 'treasure' was. He urged us all to give ourselves to that which is of real and lasting value. He chose a life of simplicity for himself. But there is one story that he told that reflects on those who do not have fellowship with the poor, the story of the rich man and Lazarus.

It was a well-known folk story, which Jesus told in a particular way. A rich man, of the worst and most ostentatious kind, and a poor man, dirty, sick and helpless, never meet in life. The rich man dines well and dresses in fine cloth. The poor man sits outside his house and his body is scarred with the sores of the street-dweller. They both die and their fortunes are reversed. The rich man goes to Hades and suffers all the torments of the damned. Lazarus rests contentedly in the bosom of Abraham. The rich man pleads for help; first for himself – some water to cool his burning tongue – and then for his relatives – someone to warn them of what awaits unless they repent. But there is no comfort for the rich. The story says that they have Moses and the prophets and that is enough. And no one, says the parable, can cross the great gulf fixed between the saved and damned. It's a story with a simple message and an easy moral, a bit like an Aesop's fable.

But the parable somehow undoes itself and offers just a shard of hope. It ends with the rich man, now suffering the torments of Hades, pleading with Abraham to let someone from the world of the dead rise again to visit his brothers to convert them. Abraham says that it's not possible and argues that anyway they will pay no heed even if someone should rise from the dead. But, of course, the Gospel-reader knows, and Luke knew as he wrote down this story, that someone *had* risen from the dead, that Jesus himself had crossed the unbridgeable chasm between the living and the dead, between the rich and the poor, that Jesus himself has shown that new life was possible when all hope seemed absolutely and for ever lost. And there were those, hundreds of new Christians, who *had* heard at last because of him the message of Moses and the prophets and had begun to build a new kind of community, in which the old divisions between people – men and women, Greek and Jew, and even rich and poor – were being set aside.

Dante once wrote that over the gates of Hell are the words, 'Abandon all hope ye who enter here.' But the witness of the Bible is that there is not anywhere, in heaven, on earth, or below, in which hope must for ever be abandoned. One of the psalms tells us that God is even in the underworld: 'If I make my bed in Sheol, you are there.'[26] God will go to hell and back to find us, and has done.

Cranmer wrote, in 'the prayer of humble access', that we are not worthy so much as to eat the crumbs from God's table. But God is merciful and kind. God gives us no scraps, but a banquet of love and hope and mercy. And Paul wrote to the church at Corinth, struggling as it was with the divide between rich and poor: 'For you know the generous act of our Lord Jesus Christ, that though he was rich, yet for your sakes he became poor, so that by his poverty you might become rich.'[27]

[26] Psalm 139.

[27] 2 Corinthians 8:9.

Conclusion

The Christian faith has always challenged the world as it is and envisaged a renewed world in which things are different. The old divides and exclusions are overcome. God becomes human. Death is defeated. Even poverty will end. And of course this is not to be accomplished by human effort alone. Christians recognise that sin is real and that, over and over again, even the best intentions fail. We know that even a church that has those in poverty in its pews can still not be *of* the poor, but ignore their voices, needs and witness, or create a culture in which they are marginalised. But the good news is that what we judge as impossible is possible with God. And repeatedly, those very things which we had thought fixed and sure are subject to change because of God's abiding love. So, from thinking that 'rich and poor' are fixed in their places by God, or to thinking that 'the poor' provide an opportunity for service, the church can come to see that we are all rich and poor, and that standing in the same place, as the one body of Christ, we can wait and work with confidence for the end of that kind of poverty which is death, violence and scandal. But we cannot find that theological wisdom and hope unless we are together and unless the church is a community in which the poor are present, heard, privileged even. For we will not know Christ if we are separated from one another. This is why if the church is to be the church, it must be a church of the poor, a church in which giving and receiving are part of life, and a church which is committed to ending poverty.

PART 3

Resources

CHURCH ACTION ON POVERTY

This resource section, compiled by Church Action on Poverty, will help your church consider how some of the issues raised in the book can be taken further. Here you find practical suggestions as well as details about key organisations and suggested further reading.

A church for the poor

'Oh, how I would like a poor Church, and for the poor.'

(Pope Francis, speaking to journalists at the Vatican on 16 March 2014)

Poverty is absolutely central to the gospel. The church is called to stand alongside anybody who is marginalised and excluded – especially people who are in poverty. Passages in scripture such as the Magnificat and the Beatitudes make it very clear that God is actively on the side of the poor:

'He has brought down the powerful from their thrones, and lifted up the lowly; he has filled the hungry with good things, and sent the rich away empty.'

(Luke 1:52–53)

'Blessed are you who are poor, for yours is the kingdom of God ... But woe to you who are rich, for you have received your comfort.'

(Luke 6:20, 24)

Traditions such as liberation theology respond to this scriptural message by talking about God's preferential 'option for the poor'. It has been very encouraging to see church leaders such as Pope Francis speaking out prophetically about this – and actually living it out in their lives and churches.

But creating a church which is of and for the poor is especially challenging in a wealthy country like the UK. Poverty here is often hidden. To be poor in the UK is to be ignored and excluded from the things that most people take for granted. People in poverty often feel they have no voice in decisions that affect them. Poverty in the UK is a source of shame; people on low incomes are routinely dismissed, stigmatised and blamed for their own situation by newspapers and politicians.

Unfortunately, many members of church congregations share the prejudices about poverty which are promoted in the media. Churches are often not the places of inclusion and welcome that they should be for people who are on low incomes or face other kinds of poverty and financial exclusion. And even when churches do attempt to respond to poverty in their communities, they may do so in ways which perpetuate the exclusion of poorer people, and do little to tackle the root causes of poverty.

Here are some key questions to ask yourself and your church leaders:

- Is the Bible's emphasis on poverty reflected in how your church is structured? In how you pray and worship?
- What kind of poverty exists in your parish or community?
- What kind of poverty exists within your congregation? Could there be hidden poverty there?
- What does your church have to offer to people in poverty?
- Is your church a place of welcome for people of all backgrounds?
- Is your church doing anything practical to tackle poverty locally or nationally? Could it do anything differently?

Let justice roll down:
including poverty in your liturgy
Take away from me the noise of your
    songs;
I will not listen to the melody of your
    harps.
But let justice roll down like waters,
and righteousness like an ever-flowing
    stream.

(Amos 5:23–24)

This is just one of the many passages about justice in the Bible. In fact, over 5,000 verses in scripture refer to issues of poverty and justice. It is arguably the strongest and most consistent theme running through the Bible, from the commandments through the prophets, to the parables and the practices of the early Church.

But how much do poverty and justice feature in our worship? How often is it the focus of our worship? And does the way we function in a church setting embody the concern for justice and inclusion that we preach?

A good place to start is with choosing hymns and prayers which reflect these concerns, and with considering them when preaching. The resources listed below are all helpful in this regard.

Resources for prayer and liturgy

- Church Action on Poverty runs an online prayer community connected to issues of poverty and inequality, and regularly produces liturgy outlines on related themes. You can find all of these at www. church-poverty.org.uk/pray.

- *Just Church*, Church Action on Poverty's free study and action programme, includes modules on worship and prayer which contain lots of advice, prayers, hymns and activities. Download them free at www. justchurch.org.uk.

- The Wild Goose Resource Group publishes many collections of prayers, hymns and liturgy outlines which reflect the Iona Community's focus on justice, peace and poverty. Find out more at www.wgrg.co.uk.

- Dancing Scarecrow is a free online collection of prayers and other materials developed by an inner-city church community in Manchester, at www.dancingscarecrow.org.uk.

- The Bible Society publish the *Poverty and Justice Bible*, which highlights all of the verses relating to these topics and includes notes, activities and discussion materials. Find out more and order a copy at www. povertyandjusticebible.org.

Tackling poverty: taking action in your community

'Hard work; but good work – because it enables us to hear voices which would not otherwise be heard.'

(Participant in 'Listen Up!', a programme delivered jointly by Church Action on Poverty and Sheffield Diocese, 2013)

Churches are often at the forefront of responses to poverty. With their direct connections to communities, they may become aware of local need before anybody else; and churches are often the only ones who are there to support the most marginalised people in our communities. A great example of this is the way that churches have responded to the explosive rise in people going hungry after 2010, by setting up food banks and other emergency projects on an enormous scale.

Unfortunately, practical projects like these run the risk of being paternalistic: viewing people in poverty as passive recipients of charity, and as 'other', outside and excluded from the church community. And while it is essential to meet people's immediate needs, the church is called to go further – to speak out prophetically when confronted with injustice, to challenge the structural causes of poverty rather than just tackling its symptoms.

Church Action on Poverty supports churches to use that prophetic voice, mobilising them to take part in campaigns which tackle the policies that trap people in poverty. We have also pioneered ways of working alongside poor communities which empower people, and help them to have a voice in the decisions which affect them.

Since the late 1990s, we have worked with churches to organise 'poverty hearings' – events where MPs and other decision-makers are invited, not to be the speakers themselves, but to listen to the stories of people who have direct experience of the issues.

Another example is the Sustainable Livelihoods approach – which we adapted for the UK from the context of international development. It addresses poverty by exploring what assets people have, rather than just looking at it as a lack of resources. By listening closely to people, we can help them identify their physical, social, political and other assets, and use them to create sustainable routes out of poverty. The same approach can be valuable for churches. Rather than asking what local need you can respond to, ask yourself what assets you have that you could share with the community. Buildings? Skills? Equipment?

In a project called 'Listen Up!', we trained churches in poor areas of Sheffield to build relationships with their communities using this Livelihoods approach. It has led to real action for change, planned jointly between the churches and local people. It was also transformational for the church members who took part:

'I have met new strangers, who have shared so much of their circumstances with me, if I had any stereotypical ideas about them, they have been blown away. And if I had any fear about getting involved with those who are really struggling and who are embedded in the culture of their estates, it has paled into insignificance at the side of their courage and their acceptance of me, and my desire to pray for them and with them.'

Useful resources for practical action

- Church Action on Poverty runs a network of e-campaigners taking action on poverty and inequality issues, produces regular reports on key topics and supplies resource packs to help churches explore the issues and support national campaigns. You can sign up or download materials at www. church-poverty.org.uk/act.

- *Just Church*, Church Action on Poverty's free study and action programme, includes modules on community and transformation. They contain useful activities and resources, such as a template for doing your own audit of your church's assets. Download them free at www.justchurch.org.uk.

- *The Sustainable Livelihoods Handbook*, published jointly by Church Action on Poverty and Oxfam, contains all the tools and information needed to use this approach with local people. It is free to download at www.church-poverty.org.uk/ livelihoods, and Church Action on Poverty can provide advice and training on how to make best use of it.

- Both the Church Urban Fund and the Methodist Church have produced online maps which can help to quantify the poverty and deprivation in your parish or community. See www.cuf.org.uk/poverty-england/ poverty-look-tool and www.methodist.org. uk/links/church-webmap-advanced-version.

Further reading on poverty and inclusion

Paul Morrison, *The Lies We Tell Ourselves: Ending comfortable myths about poverty* (Joint Public Issues Team, 2013) exposes the lies and misconceptions about poverty which are common in the UK, resourcing churches to challenge stigmatisation and exclusion.

David Rhodes, *Faith in Dark Places* (London: SPCK, 2013) explores the revolutionary idea that hope for a better world is to be found where we least expect it: among the homeless and the poor.

The Urban Theology Unit and the Contextual Theology Centre both have numerous publications which are relevant to poverty and inclusion – see www.utusheffield.org.uk and www.theology-centre.org.uk.

Index